MAN UTD LEGENDS ALPHABET

Words by Robin Feiner

A is for **A**ndy Cole. Predatory instincts and a ruthless partnership with Yorke helped secure United's historic treble winning season.

B is for George Best. A celebrity on and off the pitch, 'El Beatle' was described as the 'greatest footballer in the world' by the greatest footballer of all time, Pele.

C is for Bobby Charlton. The only Englishman to win a World Cup, European Cup and Ballon d'Or, Sir Bobby is the ultimate United legend.

D is for David Beckham. Renowned for his bending free-kicks, Becks has become a United icon and global ambassador for the sport.

E is for **Eric** Cantona. With his trademark up-turned collar and dazzling ball *skills*, this Frenchman played a key role in United's revival in the 90s. All hail King Eric.

F is for Rio Ferdinand. Regarded as one the best defenders of his generation, Ferdinand's partnership with Vidic formed Europe's finest defence.

G is for Ryan **G**iggs.
The most decorated
footballer in English
history, he set records
that will never be topped.
Giggsy is the greatest
legend among legends.

H is for Harry Gregg. With a strong presence and a safe pair of hands, Harry's heroics saving the lives of his teammates in the Munich air disaster is the stuff of legend.

**I is for Denis Irwin.
Sir Alex Ferguson once
claimed that this super-
dependable fullback would
be the only certainty in
his all-star XI.**

Jj

J is for Johnny Carey.
As versatile as they come
playing nine different
positions, Johnny captained
United to League and FA
Cup titles.

K is for Roy **K**eane. Aggressive and explosive, Keano was a wonderful reader of the game who inspired United to glory for over a decade.

L is for Denis Law. Nicknamed 'The King' by fans and 'Denis The Menace' by foes, it was Law's goal scoring feats that earned his place in United's Holy Trinity.

M is for Sir Matt Busby. For famously building the 'Busby Babes' and winning 13 trophies, Sir Matt Busby is celebrated as one of the greatest managers of all time.

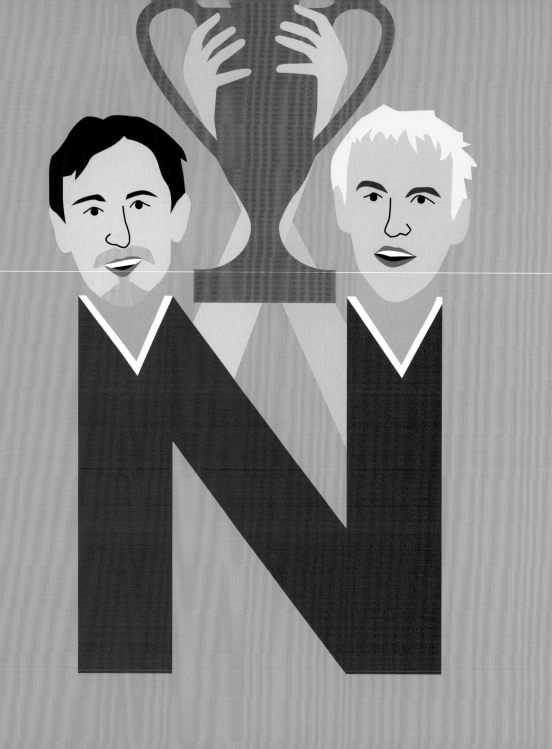

Nn

N is for Gary & Phil **N**eville. Admired for their consistency and tenacity, the Neville brothers rose from the 'Class of 92' to become the foundation of United's formidable defence.

O is for Ole Gunnar Solskjaer. The 'Baby-faced Assassin' was United's ultimate 'super-sub,' clinching historic wins with his mysterious talent for scoring last minute goals.

P is for **P**eter Schmeichel. With his commanding presence and imposing stature, the 'Great Dane' is regarded as one of the greatest goalkeepers of all time.

Q is for **Q**uinton Fortune. Growing up under apartheid, Quinton defied the odds to become the first and only South African to play for Manchester United.

R is for Cristiano **R**onaldo. Hailed as the greatest player of all time, it's Ronaldo's achievements with United that distinguish him from his rival, Messi.

S is for Paul **S**choles. As the greatest English midfielder of his generation and the most decorated English footballer of all time, Scholesy has certainly earned his place in football's Hall of Fame.

T is for Sandy **T**urnbull. As one of the original legends, Turnbull became part of United folklore scoring the very first goal at Old Trafford and the only goal in their 1909 FA Cup final win.

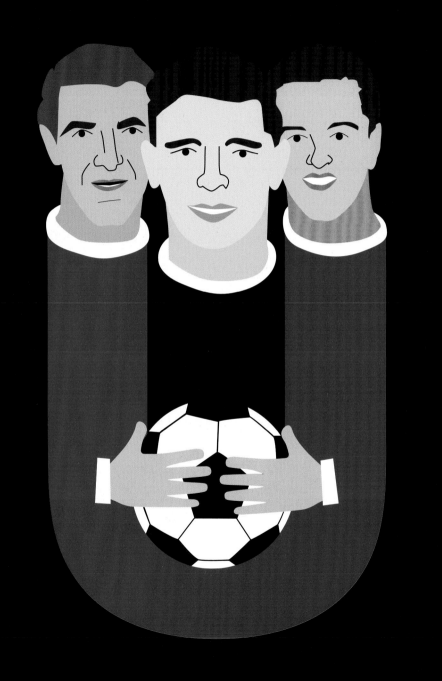

Uu

U is for 'United in Memory.' On course to winning three consecutive league titles, a legendary dynasty was tragically cut short one fateful day in February of 1958.

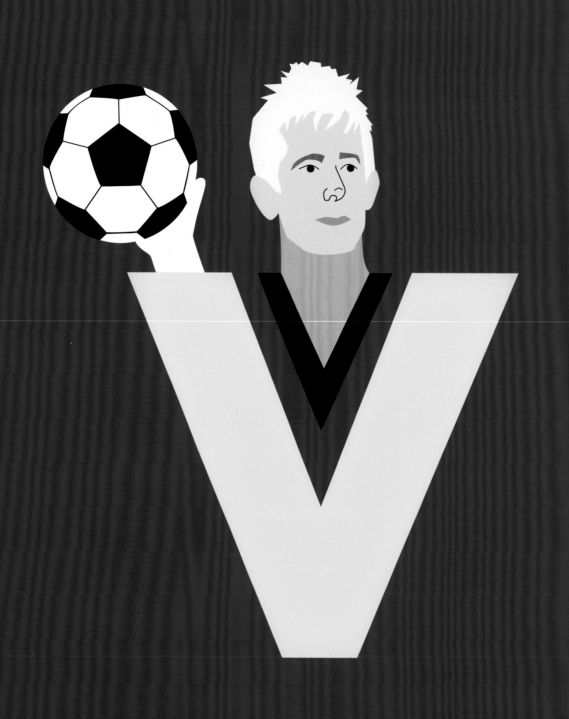

V is for Edwin van der Sar. Considered one of the best goalkeepers of all time, the towering Dutchman set many records including, 'oldest player to win the Premier League.'

Ww

W is for **W**ayne Rooney. As one of England's most accomplished players, Rooney beat Sir Bobby's long standing record to become the highest goal scorer in United's history.

X is for Alex (**X**ander) Ferguson. Sir Alex certainly possessed the 'X factor' having become the most decorated and longest serving United manager of all time.

Y is for Dwight **Y**orke. His time at United was short, but his partnership with Cole in that historic treble winning season was unforgettable.

Z is for **Z**latan Ibrahimovic. With 29 goals in only 53 games, we can only dream what might have been had this legendary striker graced Old Trafford in his prime.

UNITED STATISTICS

ANDY COLE
Years: 1995 - 2001
Appearances: 275
Goals: 121
Premier League Title: 5
FA Cup: 2
FA Charity Shield: 1
UEFA Champions
League: 1

GEORGE BEST
Years: 1963 - 1974
Appearances: 474
Goals: 181
First Division Title: 2
Charity Shield: 2
European Cup: 1

BOBBY CHARLTON
Years: 1956 - 1973
Appearances: 758
Goals: 249
First Division Title: 3
FA Cup: 1
Charity Shield: 4
European Cup: 1

DAVID BECKHAM
Years: 1992 - 2003
Appearances: 394
Goals: 85
Premier League Title: 6
FA Cup: 2
FA Community Shield: 2
UEFA Champions
League: 1
Intercontinental Cup: 1

ERIC CANTONA
Years: 1992 - 1997
Appearances: 185
Goals: 82
Premier League Title: 4
FA Cup: 2
Charity Shield: 3

RIO FERDINAND
Years: 2002 - 2014
Appearances: 455
Goals: 8
Premier League Title: 6
Football League Cup: 2
FA Community Shield: 4
UEFA Champions
League: 1
FIFA Club World Cup: 1

RYAN GIGGS
Years: 1990 - 2014
Appearances: 963
Goals: 168
Premier League Title: 13
FA Cup: 4
Football League Cup: 3
FA Community Shield: 9
UEFA Champions
League: 2
UEFA Super Cup: 1
Intercontinental Cup: 1
FIFA Club World Cup: 1

HARRY GREGG
Years: 1957 - 1966
Appearances: 247

DENIS IRWIN
Years: 1990 - 2002
Appearances: 529
Goals: 33
Premier League Title: 7
FA Cup: 3
Football League Cup: 1
Charity Shield: 5
UEFA Champions
League: 1
Cup Winners' Cup: 1
European Super Cup: 1
Intercontinental Cup: 1

JOHNNY CAREY
Years: 1936 - 1953
Appearances: 344
Goals: 17
First Division Title: 1
FA Cup: 1
FA Charity Shield: 1

ROY KEANE
Years: 1993 - 2005
Appearances: 480
Goals: 51
Premier League Title: 7
FA Cup: 4
FA Community Shield: 4
UEFA Champions
League: 1
Intercontinental Cup: 1

DENIS LAW
Years: 1962 - 1973
Appearances: 404
Goals: 237
First Division Title: 2
FA Cup: 1
Charity Shield: 2
European Cup: 1

SIR MATT BUSBY
Years: 1945 - 1969
First Division Title: 5
FA Cup: 2
FA Charity Shield: 5
European Cup: 1

PHIL NEVILLE
Years: 1994 - 2005
Appearances: 386
Goals: 8
Premier League Title: 6
FA Cup: 3
FA Community Shield: 3
UEFA Champions
League: 1
Intercontinental Cup: 1

GARY NEVILLE
Years: 1992-2011
Appearances: 602
Goals: 7
Premier League Title: 8
FA Cup: 3
Football League Cup: 2
FA Community Shield: 3
UEFA Champions
League: 2
Intercontinental Cup: 1
FIFA Club World Cup: 1

OLE GUNNAR SOLSKJAER
Years: 1996 - 2007
Appearances: 366
Goals: 126
Premier League Title: 6
FA Cup: 2
FA Community Shield: 2
UEFA Champions
League: 1
Intercontinental Cup: 1

PETER SCHMEICHEL
Years: 1991 - 1999
Appearances: 398
Goals: 1
Premier League Title: 5
FA Cup: 3
Football League Cup: 1
FA Charity Shield: 4
UEFA Champions
League: 1
UEFA Super Cup: 1

QUINTON FORTUNE
Years: 1999 - 2006
Appearances: 126
Goals: 11
Premier League Title: 1
FA Community Shield: 1
Intercontinental Cup: 1

CRISTIANO RONALDO
Years: 2003 - 2009
Appearances: 292
Goals: 118
Premier League Title: 3
FA Cup: 1
Football League Cup: 2
FA Community Shield: 1
UEFA Champions
League: 1
FIFA Club World Cup: 1

PAUL SCHOLES
Years: 1993 - 2013
Appearances: 718
Goals: 155
Premier League Title: 11
FA Cup: 3
Football League Cup: 2
FA Community Shield: 5
UEFA Champions
League: 2
Intercontinental Cup: 1
FIFA Club World Cup: 1

SANDY TURNBULL
Years: 1906 - 1915
Appearances: 247
Goals: 101
First Division Title: 2
FA Cup: 1

LEGENDS OF THE 'MUNICH AIR DISASTER'

Duncan Edwards
Tommy Taylor
Roger Byrne
Geoff Bent
Eddie Colman
Mark Jones
David Pegg
Liam "Billy" Whelan

EDWIN VAN DER SAR

Years: 2005 - 2011
Appearances: 266
Premier League Title: 4
Football League Cup: 2
FA Community Shield: 3
UEFA Champions
League: 1
FIFA Club World Cup: 1

WAYNE ROONEY

Years: 2004 - 2017
Appearances: 559
Goals: 253
Premier League Title: 5
FA Cup: 1
Football League Cup: 3
FA Community Shield: 4
UEFA Champions
League: 1
UEFA Europa League: 1
FIFA Club World Cup: 1

ALEX (XANDER) FERGUSON

Years: 1986 - 2013
Premier League Title: 13
FA Cup: 5
Football League Cup: 4
FA Charity/Community
Shield: 10
UEFA Champions
League: 2
UEFA Cup Winners' Cup: 1
UEFA Super Cup: 1
Intercontinental Cup: 1
FIFA Club World Cup: 1

DWIGHT YORKE

Years: 1998 - 2002
Appearances: 147
Goals: 65
Premier League Title: 3
FA Cup: 1
UEFA Champions
League: 1
Intercontinental Cup: 1

ZLATAN IBRAHIMOVIĆĆ

Years: 2016 - 2018
Appearances: 53
Goals: 29
EFL Cup: 1
UEFA Europa League: 1
FA Community Shield: 1

MAN UTD LEGENDS ALPHABET
www.alphabetlegends.com

Published by Alphabet Legends Pty Ltd in 2018
Created by Beck Feiner
Copyright © Alphabet Legends Pty Ltd 2018

978-0-6482616-1-2

**EXPLORE THESE LEGENDARY ALPHABETS
& MORE AT WWW.ALPHABETLEGENDS.COM**

ALPHABET LEGENDS